D1707087

A LIVING GRAMMAR

By
WINIFRED WATSON
and
JULIUS M. NOLTE

Drawings by
SHIZU MATSUDA

AVENEL BOOKS • NEW YORK

Preface

WHEN THIS LITTLE VOLUME was first published in 1938, the authors regarded it as experimental. They realized that the book could not pretend to be a "text" in the academic sense, that its contents were not specifically tailored for a particular age group, and that in attempting to approach the subject from the point of view of the young "consumer" of grammar it might not fulfill any valuable educational purpose.

In presenting a fifth revision, the authors offer it in the same spirit which characterized their attitude in 1938. It has been difficult to resist the temptation to make this more comprehensive and to add material on many other aspects of grammatical and rhetorical usage. But the true philosophy of the book, the authors believe, is what it was in the beginning, namely to be vivid rather than exhaustive. The book deals suggestively with a few fundamentals, and simplicity is its keynote. The authors are fully aware today, as they were in 1938, that when you simplify you tend to broaden generalizations and that when you broaden a generalization you invite argument among the pundits. Well, the authors aren't interested in the pundits, but in the adventures of ordinary people with the English language, and as to their book they can urge with assurance : Try it.

Contents

A LIVING GRAMMAR

" . . . beginneth not with obscure definitions which must blur the margin with interpretations and load the memory with doubtfulness."

—SIR PHILIP SIDNEY

Why keep grammar in the horse-and-buggy days?

Let's bring it up-to-date!

i

The Parts of Speech

"Who climbs the Grammar tree distinctly knows
Where Noun and Verb and Participle grows."
—John Dryden

REMEMBER,

when you go to the library, that there are only *eight kinds of words* in all those books!

No matter what you read, what you say, or what you write, you use only *eight kinds of words*. There are no more.

These words are called THE PARTS OF SPEECH.

THE PARTS OF SPEECH are:

NOUNS, PRONOUNS, VERBS, ADJECTIVES, ADVERBS,

PREPOSITIONS, CONJUNCTIONS, INTERJECTIONS.

You will remember them easily if you learn this poem:

NOUNS are just the names of things,

As *rice*, and *birds*,

and *snow*, and *rings*.

The ARTICLES* are *the, a, an;*

They point out nouns: *the* boy,

a man.

PRONOUNS take the place of nouns,

As *she* for woman, *they* for clowns.

---

*Articles are one kind of adjective.

ADJECTIVES describe the nouns,

As *quacking* ducks,

and *pretty* gowns.

The VERB some action names, like *stir;*
Or state, like *is,* or *was,* or *were.*

Something is done: the ADVERBS then
Tell *how* and *why* and *where* and *when.*

A PREPOSITION precedes a noun:
By, at, from, to, or *in* the town.

And, or, and *but* join words and clauses,
CONJUNCTIONS — used instead of pauses.

Strong-feeling words are *Ouch!* and *Oh!*
They're INTERJECTIONS: *Ah! Bah! Lo!*

ii

ii

The Noun

NOUNS are just the names of things,
As *rice,* and *snow,* and *birds,* and *rings.*

The NOUN!

Isn't that something?

Yes, it is!

It is the name of something.

NOUNS *name* things.

The *name* of anything you can think of is a NOUN.

A,

   An,

      The,

         are like three little pigs.

They just tag along with nouns.

We call them ARTICLES.

ARTICLES are one kind of adjective.*

      a dog   *an* apple   *the* candy

---

*Adjectives are explained on page 29.

ARTICLES can *always* be used with nouns.

To test a word, put an *article* (*a, an, the*) before it.
If the word is a *noun* it makes sense with an article.

song	*a* song
artist	*an* artist
man	*the* man

From this test we know that *song, artist,* and *man*
are nouns.

Read, sat, eat, are not nouns. How do we know?

When do we use *a* and when do we use *an?* Most
nouns beginning with the letters *a, e, i, o, u,*
insist upon *an.*

They want nothing to do with the article *a.*

an onion	not	*a* onion
an umpire	not	*a* umpire

Nouns that do not begin with these letters prefer *a.*

a horse	not	*an* horse
a flower	not	*an* flower

A few nouns are contrary. For instance:

      an hour   *a* union   *an* X-ray   *a* university

"The Billy Goat would like to chew
Your picture book or shirt or shoe;
His whiskers wriggle on his chin.
He doesn't really swallow tin,
But eats the laundry off the line,
And likes the taste of sticks and twine.

The Nanny Goat is Billy's bride;
They chew the laundry side by side."

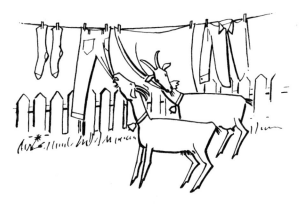

About the only things that the goats didn't eat are
the nouns. Can you find them?

NOUNS are of two kinds: COMMON and PROPER.

COMMON NOUNS name one or more of a class of
objects that are alike.

dog	mice
book	snakes
girl	fishes

For example, there is a large class of
animals called *dogs*.

When we say *dog* we mean one of
the animals in this large class
called dogs.

Dog is a COMMON NOUN.

We can also say *dogs*, meaning four dogs, four hundred dogs, or any number of dogs of this class.

Dogs is a COMMON NOUN.

PROPER NOUNS are the special names given to certain persons, places, or things.

God	John	Minnesota
Lord	Mary	New York

Many of our grammatical terms come from Latin words.*

Proper comes from a Latin word *proprius,* meaning *belonging to one.*

A PROPER NOUN is a name that *belongs to one.*

More PROPER NOUNS:

Persons { John
          Mary

Places { Arizona
         California

Things { Bellevue Hospital
         New York Times

It is proper to begin a PROPER NOUN with a capital letter.

---

*Many years ago, when English was a young language, most writing was in Latin, which was then a languge used throughout Europe. English grammar was first explained by using Latin words first applied to Latin grammar. These

There are several *classes* of COMMON NOUNS.

The names of things that we can see, hear, touch, smell, and taste, such as *picture, music, book, odor,* or *candy,* are called

CONCRETE or MATERIAL NOUNS

We can get to them instantly through one or more of the five senses.

But there are some things that cannot be reached so easily, things like *beauty, flock,* or *skating.*

Such nouns also have special names. Among them are:

ABSTRACT NOUNS

COLLECTIVE NOUNS

VERBAL NOUNS

Latin words finally became part of our English language. Many of them are still used in grammar books. In this grammar book some of these Latin words are explained. When we understand them, we shall remember them more easily.

ABSTRACT NOUNS name *qualities.*

beauty	honesty	envy
love	solitude	anger
truth	unity	grief

COLLECTIVE NOUNS are names applied to *groups* or *collections* of people or things that are alike or are related.

crowd	flock
group	multitude
congregation	dozen

VERBAL NOUNS are verb forms used as nouns.

Seeing is *believing.*
Skiing thrills me.
Sliding is fun.

A noun has NUMBER.

If it refers to **1** it is SINGULAR.

one hat

one box

If it refers to **2 or more** it is PLURAL.

two hats

three books

four bottles

Take a number from 2 to 9,999,999.
Every one of these numbers is PLURAL!

1 is the only number that is SINGULAR.

A noun has GENDER.

GENDER means *kind*.

There are THREE GENDERS:

    MASCULINE

    FEMININE

    NEUTER

MASCULINE nouns are the names of male beings.

FEMININE nouns are the names of female beings.

NEUTER nouns are the names of *things*. *Neuter* means *neither*. NEUTER nouns are *neither* masculine nor feminine.

Examples:

MASCULINE	FEMININE	NEUTER
king	queen	throne
man	woman	house
boy	girl	picture
lion	lioness	jungle

NEUTER nouns are sometimes thought of as having gender.

We speak of the moon as feminine:

   "The moon shines in all her splendor."

We speak of the sun as masculine:

   "The sun sheds his light upon us."

WHY?

Here's the answer:

Long ago people worshipped the sun as a god; the moon as a goddess.

We no longer worship the sun and moon as god and goddess, but we still speak of them as masculine and feminine.

A noun has CASE.

We know about cases of measles, mumps, and chicken-pox.

And we know about law cases, bookcases, watchcases, and spectacle cases.

So, too, there are CASES in grammar.

In grammar, CASE expresses the relation a noun or pronoun has to other words in the sentence.

Nouns and pronouns are the only words that have CASE.

To understand CASE, it is necessary to know what a sentence is.

A SENTENCE is a thought expressed in words. It has two parts: SUBJECT and PREDICATE.

The SUBJECT names the person or thing *talked about.*

The PREDICATE tells what is said *about the subject.*

And now we get down to CASES.

There are THREE CASES in English grammar:

The NOMINATIVE CASE names the *subject* of the sentence. Let's represent it by a brief-case, for subject-matter.

The OBJECTIVE CASE names the *object* of verb or preposition.* Think of it as a stout packing-case, for objects.

The POSSESSIVE CASE shows ownership. When we know there are valuables about and want to know who the owner is, the POSSESSIVE CASE tells us. A safe may well represent the POSSESSIVE CASE.

---

*Don't worry about verbs and prepositions. We'll come to them later, on pages 37 and 70.

The NOMINATIVE CASE names the subject.

The SUBJECT is what the sentence talks about.

> The *grass* is green.
>
> The *frog* jumped.
>
> The *man* sang loudly.
>
> The *fire* died down.
>
> The *pig* squealed.
>
> *Scotland* was burning.

Remember: The NOMINATIVE is the *name* CASE.

What are we talking about?

The *subject,* of course.

The OBJECTIVE CASE sometimes answers the question, "*What?*" after the verb.

The girl baked a cake.

The girl baked *what?*
Cake answers the question, "*What?*"
Therefore *cake* is in the OBJECTIVE CASE.

The OBJECTIVE CASE sometimes answers the question, "*Whom?*" after the verb.

The boy beat the man at horseshoes.

The boy beat *whom?*
Man answers the question, "*Whom?*"
Therefore *man* is in the OBJECTIVE CASE.

The DIRECT OBJECT answers the question, "*What?*" or "*Whom?*" after the verb.

The DIRECT OBJECT is sometimes called the OBJECT COMPLEMENT.

OBJECTS OF PREPOSITIONS are also in the OBJECTIVE CASE. This use of the OBJECTIVE CASE is explained on page 72.

A noun or pronoun that answers the question,
"*Whose?*" is in the POSSESSIVE CASE.

The dog chased Smith's cat.

This is my country.

Andy's goat broke loose.

She ate her spinach.

Hiram's horse needs shoes.

Their fireplace smokes.

She disobeyed the doctor's orders.

The airplane swooped down over Higgins'
pasture.

All the words that answer the question, "*Whose?*"
in these sentences are in the POSSESSIVE CASE.

The POSSESSIVE *possesses.*

The POSSESSIVE CASE *points out* the owner.

NOUNS IN A NUTSHELL

The facts about the nouns are few.

Here they are in brief review:

There are two kinds
{ common
  proper

They have number
{ singular
  plural

They have gender
{ masculine
  feminine
  neuter

They have case
{ nominative
  objective
  possessive

The Pronoun

PRONOUNS take the place of nouns,
As *she* for woman, *they* for clowns.

Take Grammar to the movies!

You have heard of a movie stand-in.

A PRONOUN is a stand-in for a noun.

Pro, in Latin, means *for* or *in place of.*

A PRONOUN stands *for* or *in place of* a noun.

PRONOUNS are used to avoid tiresome repetition of nouns.

What is the matter with this?

> Carrie left home this morning, didn't Carrie? Carrie first ate Carrie's breakfast. Then Carrie took Carrie's books and put Carrie's hat on Carrie's head. Carrie looked at Carrie's mother's clock and saw that the time was 8:45. Carrie's mother told Carrie not to be late for school.

There are *too many Carries!*

How would you say it?

You would put other words in place of Carrie.

These words are PRONOUNS.

PRONOUNS have ANTECEDENTS.

In Latin, *ante* means *before; cedere* means *to go.*

Antecedent means *that which goes before.*

The noun for which the PRONOUN stands is the ANTECEDENT.

Mary looked at her reflection
in the mirror.

Mary is the ANTECEDENT of the PRONOUN *her.*

What are the ANTECEDENTS of the pronouns in the following sentences?

> George carried the book across the room
> and put it in the bookshelf.

> John came into the warming house and took
> off his skates.

> It's time for the river to overflow its banks.*

---

*For the difference between *it's* and *its* see page 91.

Pronouns that tell

> who is speaking,
> who is being spoken to,
> who is being spoken of,
> or
> what is being spoken of,

are called PERSONAL PRONOUNS.

> *He* spoke to *her* about *it*.

The PERSONAL PRONOUNS are *I, you, he, she, it,** and their various forms, listed on page 26.

———

*Sometimes we use *it* without an antecedent, as in:
> *It* is time to go to school.
> *It* is raining.
When used in this way, *it* is called an IMPERSONAL PRONOUN.

PERSONAL PRONOUNS, like nouns, have number, gender, and case.

They also have another characteristic which we call PERSON.

PERSON is the relation the pronoun has to the speaker or writer of the sentence.

There are THREE PERSONS:

FIRST PERSON: the person *speaking.*

SECOND PERSON: the person *spoken to.*

THIRD PERSON: the person or thing *spoken of.*

Memorize this sentence:

I am speaking to *you* about *him.*

HE = THIRD PERSON

SHE = THIRD PERSON

YOU = SECOND PERSON

I = FIRST PERSON

This table will help you to keep the relationships of
the PERSONAL PRONOUNS straight:

Person	Nominative Case	Objective Case	Possessive Case	Gender
Singular				
First	I	me	my mine	*Masculine or Feminine*
Second	you	you	your, yours	*Masculine or Feminine*
Third	he she	him her	his her hers	*Masculine, Feminine*
	it	it	its	*Neuter*
Plural				
First	we	us	our ours	*Masculine or Feminine*
Second	you ye	you	your yours	*Masculine or Feminine*
Third	they	them	their theirs	*Masculine, Feminine or Neuter*

A PRONOUN agrees with its antecedent in person,
number, and gender.

A PRONOUN that points to or points out is called a
DEMONSTRATIVE PRONOUN.

This, that, these, and *those* are DEMONSTRATIVE PRO-
NOUNS.

> Here is a nice hat. I will take *this.*
> *That* is the man I mean.
> Of all my books, I like *these* best.

A pronoun that reflects or points back to the subject is called a REFLEXIVE PRONOUN.

The REFLEXIVE PRONOUNS are *myself, yourself, him-
self, herself, itself, ourselves, yourselves,* and *themselves.*

> The boy hurt *himself.*

A pronoun that points out but does not say who is
called an INDEFINITE PRONOUN.

The INDEFINITE PRONOUNS are *one, any, some,* and
such compounds as *anyone* and *someone.*

> *One* should do the best *one* can.
> Is *anyone* at home?

A pronoun introducing a clause which describes an antecedent is called a RELATIVE PRONOUN.

Who, which, what and *that* are RELATIVE PRONOUNS.

The man *who* ran arrived first.

Who is a relative pronoun. It introduces the clause *who ran,* describing its antecedent, *man.*

When the pronouns *who, which, what,* are used to ask questions, they are called INTERROGATIVE PRONOUNS.

Who is your favorite author?
Which is your hat?
What did you say?

Remember the INTERROGATIVE PRONOUN as the owl pronoun.

Which?

What?

Who? Who? Who?

iv

The Adjective

ADJECTIVES describe the nouns,
As *quacking* ducks, and *pretty* gowns.

ADJECTIVES are gossips!
They "tell on" *nouns* and
pronouns.

Ad, in Latin, means *to* or *at.*

Iacere, in Latin, means to *throw* or *hurl.*

An ADJECTIVE is a word that is *thrown at* another
word.

We throw ADJECTIVES at nouns and pronouns.

Why?

To give a clearer picture of the noun or pronoun.

29

An ADJECTIVE's work is to *modify* a noun or pronoun.

Modify sometimes means to *change* or *alter*.
It also means to *classify*, to *show type or kind*.

a day
a rainy day   }   *Rainy* modifies day.

a person   }   *Sick* alters the meaning of the
a sick person }   word *person*.

The girl cried.   } *Beautiful* classifies the word
The beautiful girl }   girl. (She belongs to the
    cried.   }   *class* of beautiful girls.)

Rainy, sick, beautiful are ADJECTIVES. They *modify*
nouns.

Modify also means to *limit*.

Consider the noun *dogs*. Let it represent all the dogs in the world. Let us suppose these dogs are pictured below.

There are *big* dogs and *little* dogs; *short-haired* dogs and *long-haired* dogs; *black* dogs, *white* dogs, *brown* dogs, and *spotted* dogs.

Now let us say *black* dogs. We at once limit the dogs we are talking about to the black dogs and must disregard all other kinds.

So here we have all the black dogs.

But some of these black dogs are short-haired, some
are long-haired. Let us say black, long-haired dogs.
We immediately limit our dogs again. There are
fewer black, long-haired dogs.

So we may continue to limit these black, long-haired
dogs to those which are small or to those which
are large.

Adjectives can be used to limit dogs in any way we
wish, even to naming the only dog of its kind in
the world!

The little, long-eared, playful
Cocker spaniel is my dog,
Ginger.

Of course, adjectives can be used to modify any noun
in a similar way.

An ADJECTIVE cannot stand alone in a sentence.

> It is a beautiful
>
> *Beautiful* is an adjective, but it doesn't make sense because it has no noun or pronoun. The sentence must name a beautiful something.

> It is a beautiful day.
>
> Now the sentence makes sense.

A test:

> A word is an ADJECTIVE if it makes sense with the word *thing* or *being.*
>
> | | |
> |---|---|
> | sweet | thing |
> | sour | thing |
> | gracious | being |
> | friendly | being |

Sweet, sour, gracious, friendly are ADJECTIVES.

Adjectives may show the *degree* or *extent* to which
the nouns they modify possess the quality the adjectives describe.

The POSITIVE FORM of the adjective is the *simple*
form.

> The bundle is *heavy*.

> *Heavy* is the POSITIVE or simple form of the
> adjective *heavy*.

The COMPARATIVE FORM of the adjective is used when
two things (no more, no less) are compared.

> This bundle is *heavier* than that bundle.

> *Heavier* is the COMPARATIVE form of the
> adjective *heavy*. One bundle has more
> "heaviness" than the other bundle.

The SUPERLATIVE FORM of the adjective is used when
three or more things are compared.

> This bundle is *heaviest* (of three, four,
> or more).

> *Heaviest* is the SUPERLATIVE form of the
> adjective *heavy*. One bundle has more
> "heaviness" than any of the other bundles
> talked about.

In most cases, in words of one and two syllables, the comparative is formed by adding *r* or *er* to the positive form.

fine	finer
small	smaller

With such words the superlative is formed by adding *st* or *est*.

finest
smallest

Rarely in words of two syllables, but *always* in words of more than two, the comparative and superlative degrees are formed by using *more* and *most* and *less* and *least* with the positive form—

more intelligent
most intelligent
less intelligent
least intelligent

Some adjectives are compared irregularly:

POSITIVE	COMPARATIVE	SUPERLATIVE
good	better	best
bad	worse	worst

What? *no* comparative or superlative?

Some adjectives have only the positive form.

When we have said,

"The bucket is full,"

we have said all that can be said.

If the bucket is *full,*
    it cannot be *fuller,*
            or *fullest.*

If the bucket is *empty,*
    it cannot be *less empty,*
            or *least empty.*

Other adjectives which do not have comparative and superlative degrees are:

whole
final
finished
perfect

v

The Verb

The VERB some action names, like *stir;*
Or state, like *is,* or *was,* or *were.*

Verb comes from a Latin word, *verbum,* meaning
word.

The VERB is a very important word.

Without a VERB there can be no sentence.

A VERB is a word which means

to do

or

to be.

The VERB makes the sentence *go!*

Here are some cars.

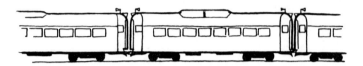

Here is a train.

If we put ten cars or a hundred cars on the track we
would not have a train.

To have a train, we must have an engine.

By adding an engine to the cars we have a train.

The VERB is the *engine of a sentence.*

The engine of the sentence does not have to be at the end.

Polly drives a car.

Drives is the engine of this sentence.

Drives is a VERB.

The day was Christmas.

Was is the engine of this sentence.

Was is a VERB.

Some sentences have two or more engines.

The children laughed and shouted at the circus.

Laughed and *shouted* are the engines of the sentence. They are both VERBS.

Most verbs are *action words*.

The pig squeals.
A horse runs.
A mule kicks.
A fire burns.
The door opens.
The sun sets.
The dog barks.

To be a verb, a word must make sense with a personal
   pronoun.

Test the word *sing*.

                              I sing.

   Sing is a verb.

Test the word *candlestick*.

                              I candlestick

   Candlestick is not a verb.

Why?

Verbs may be TRANSITIVE or INTRANSITIVE.

Transitive comes from a Latin word, *transire* meaning *to go across, to pass over.*

A TRANSITIVE VERB is a verb that carries the action from one place, person, or thing to another place, person, or thing.

The boy flies a kite.

Flies is a TRANSITIVE VERB. It tells of an action that *goes across* or *carries over* from the subject, *boy,* to the direct object, *kite.*

A TRANSITIVE VERB *must* have a direct object.

In, in combination with other words, often means *not.*

An INTRANSITIVE VERB is a verb that is *not transitive.*

An INTRANSITIVE VERB is a verb that carries *no* action from one place, person, or thing to another place, person, or thing.

The rabbits ran.

Ran is an INTRANSITIVE VERB. It carries over no action from one thing to another.

An INTRANSITIVE VERB makes sense without an object.

Verbs are fickle.

Some verbs are transitive at some times, intransitive at other times.

He grows.

No action is carried over.

Grows is *intransitive.*

She grows pumpkins.

In this sentence the action is carried from the subject *she* to the direct object *pumpkins. Grows* is *transitive.*

There are comp*li*ments and comp*le*ments.

A compliment is something said in praise of another person and has nothing to do with grammar.

A complement is a word that *completes* and has something to do with grammar.

There are two kinds of COMPLEMENTS:

> The OBJECT COMPLEMENT, which is the same as the DIRECT OBJECT, described on page 18.

> The ATTRIBUTE COMPLEMENT.

ATTRIBUTE means a *quality*.

The ATTRIBUTE COMPLEMENT may be either a *noun* (PREDICATE NOUN or PREDICATE NOMINATIVE) or an *adjective* (PREDICATE ADJECTIVE).

> He is *fearless*.

The word *fearless* tells us that *he* has the *quality* of fearlessness.

The word *fearless* attributes the quality of fearlessness to him. It *completes* what is said about the subject.

Fearless is the ATTRIBUTE COMPLEMENT.

Fearless is an adjective.

Therefore, *fearless* is a PREDICATE ADJEC-TIVE.

He is a *man*.

This sentence means that *he* has the attributes or qualities of a *man*.

Man is the ATTRIBUTE COMPLEMENT.

Man is a noun.

Therefore, *man* is a PREDICATE NOUN or PREDICATE NOMINATIVE. It is in the nominative case.

If grammar were arithmetic, these sentences might be written thus:

He = fearless.

He = man.

An ATTRIBUTE COMPLEMENT is always used when the verb is equivalent to an equals (=) sign.

Verbs in common usage which are equivalent to an equals (=) sign are called copulative verbs and are listed on page 56.

Hear ye, hear ye, hear ye!

Verbs have VOICE.

There are TWO VOICES in grammar.

They are:

The ACTIVE VOICE

The PASSIVE VOICE

Grammar is a matter of relationships.

VOICE tells the *relation* of the *subject* to the *verb*.

The verb is in the ACTIVE VOICE *when the subject does the acting.*

> Mary *made* the cake and the girls and
> boys *ate* it.

> Mary and the boys and girls *acted upon* the
> cake. The verbs *made* and *ate* are in the
> ACTIVE VOICE.

The verb is in the PASSIVE VOICE *when the subject is acted upon.*

> The cake *was made* by Mary and *was
> eaten* by the boys and girls.

> The subject, *cake, was acted upon.* There-
> fore, the verbs, *was made* and *was eaten,*
> are in the PASSIVE VOICE.

The march of time!

Verbs have TENSE.

The verb tells not only the action but the time of the
action.

The *time of the action* we call
TENSE.

Tense comes from a Latin word, *tempus*, meaning
time.

There are THREE SIMPLE TENSES:

> PRESENT TENSE Time *marches* on.
>
> PAST TENSE   Time *marched* on.
>
> FUTURE TENSE   Time *will march* on.

Picture *time* as an *open book.*

The page before you is PRESENT.

The pages to the left are PAST.

The pages to the right are FUTURE.

To understand TENSE, say to yourself:

"The PRESENT and I are always together."

Let's call the PRESENT, *now*.

Say to yourself, and think of it for a few seconds:

"I am always in the *now*.

"I can send my *mind* into the
past or into the future just
as a ventriloquist can seem to
send his voice to the lips of
his dummy. But *I am always
in the now*.

"I stay in the PRESENT, the
now."

Sometimes the sentence speaks as at the present moment; sometimes as at a moment in the past; sometimes as at a moment in the future.

"I am sailing a boat."

I am talking about the PRESENT time, the *now*, when I am actually sailing a boat.

"I sailed a boat."

This is the story of a journey my mind is making to the PAST, back to the time when I actually sailed the boat in what was *then* the PRESENT.

"I shall fly."

This is the story of a journey my mind is making forward into the FUTURE, to the time when I shall actually fly in what will *then* be the PRESENT.

An exercise in SIMPLE tenses:

PAST	PRESENT	FUTURE
I *baked* a cake.	I *bake* a cake.	I *shall bake* a cake.

Write sentences using the PAST, PRESENT, and FUTURE tenses of the verbs *bake, run, skate,* with the pronouns *you, he, she, it, they.*

There are three other tenses of the verb, often known as PROGRESSIVE tenses, which are as follows:

PAST PROGRESSIVE*	PRESENT PROGRESSIVE	FUTURE PROGRESSIVE
I *was baking* a cake.	I *am baking* a cake.	I *shall be baking* a cake.

There are also two lesser used tenses called EMPHATIC tenses, which are:

PAST EMPHATIC	PRESENT EMPHATIC
I *did bake* a cake.	I *do bake* a cake.

---

*Also called the IMPERFECT tense.

There are more tenses called the PERFECT TENSES. They are:

> The PAST PERFECT
> The PRESENT PERFECT
> The FUTURE PERFECT

In grammar, *perfect* means *finished* or *completed*.

The PAST PERFECT TENSE means that the action spoken of *was already finished* at some moment in the past.*

The PRESENT PERFECT TENSE means that the action spoken of *is already finished* at the present moment.

The FUTURE PERFECT TENSE means that, at some moment in the future, the action spoken of *will already be complete.*

Imperfect in grammar means *not completed.*
The IMPERFECT TENSE means that at some time in the past an action was *going on and on.*
The IMPERFECT TENSE is a past tense of the verb.

All that the PERFECT TENSE implies is that the action *was completed, is completed,* or *is to be completed* by the time the sentence speaks.

I *had baked* a cake.

I am speaking *now,* but the sentence speaks of a *past* time. We know that *the action of baking* was complete at that time. Therefore, *had baked* is in the PAST PERFECT TENSE.

I *have baked* a cake.

Here *I* am speaking in the *present* about the *present.* We know that the *action of baking* is over *now.* Therefore, *have baked* is in the PRESENT PERFECT TENSE.

I *shall have baked* a cake.

Here *I* speak in the *present* but the sentence speaks about a *future* time when the baking will have been completed. Therefore, *shall have baked* is in the FUTURE PERFECT TENSE.

Why should anyone be tense about TENSE?

The verb *be* has many disguises!

Sometimes *be* appears in the forms

> *am,*
> *are,*
> *is,*
> *was,*
> *were,*
> or
> *been.*

Don't let these disguises fool you.

Each one is the *be* verb in another form.

The verb *be* in any of its guises *affirms existence.*

> I *am* a man.
> (I affirm that I exist as a man.)

> God *is.*
> (It is affirmed that God exists.)

The verb *be,* in all its forms, is usually used as a
COPULA.

A COPULA *couples* or *links.*

A COPULA links a *subject* with a *predicate adjective*
or a *predicate noun.*

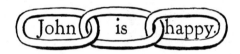

> *Is* is the COPULA which links or couples the
> subject, *John,* with the predicate adjec-
> tive, *happy.*
>
> The baby *is* Carol.

Is is the COPULA which couples the subject,
baby, with the predicate noun, *Carol.*

When *be,* in any of its forms, is used as a COPULA it
is called a COPULATIVE VERB or LINKING VERB.*

Other verbs are sometimes used as COPULAS. Among
them are:

appear	look	seem	taste
smell	feel	become	sound

---

*The verb *be* in its various forms may also be used as a principal
verb.

     I *am.*   Carthage *was.*

These verbs may *couple* or *link* subject with attribute.

The rose *smells* sweet.

Smells is a COPULATIVE VERB coupling the subject, *rose,* with the predicate adjective, *sweet.*

Tell what the COPULATIVE VERBS link in these sentences:

The dog looked ill.
The cloth feels rough.
The lad seems grown.
The pill tastes bitter.
The dress became worn.

Subject and predicate noun and subject and predicate adjective refer to the *same thing.*

He is John.
Candy tastes sweet.

The subject and the direct object, however, always refer to *different things.*

Mary chased the cat.

The COPULA *be* and other COPULATIVE VERBS are *intransitive.*

Mood means *temper, state, disposition.*

A mood is a frame of mind.

People are temperamental and have different *moods* at different times.

Verbs also are temperamental!

Verbs, like people, have moods.

In grammar, MODE is the same as MOOD.

In grammar, MODE means *class* or *state.*

The verb has *three* MODES. They are:

The INDICATIVE MODE, which expresses a plain statement of fact.

The SUBJUNCTIVE MODE, which deals with statements that are less than fact.

The IMPERATIVE MODE, which states a command or entreaty.

The INDICATIVE MODE deals with facts.

The INDICATIVE MODE either *asserts* something as a
fact, or *inquires* after the fact.

America is the land of a free people.

Are tomatoes fruit?

The SUBJUNCTIVE MODE deals, not with facts, but with

> wishes,
> possibilities, or
> expressions contrary to fact.

Sub means *below.*

Subway means a *way below* the surface.

The SUBJUNCTIVE MODE is used when a statement is *below* or *less than* a fact.

> I wish that he would come.
>
> Would that I were President!
>
> If he were living he would have written.
>
> If wishes were fishes we might have some fried.

The SUBJUNCTIVE MODE is almost always introduced by one of these conjunctions*: *if, though, lest, unless, till, until, whether,* or by a verb of wishing, such as *would* or *wish.* (But words following these conjunctions or verbs are not *always* in the subjunctive mode; they may be in the indicative.)

---

*Read about conjunctions on page 76.

Imperative comes from the Latin word, *imperare.*

It means *to rule, to command.*

The IMPERATIVE MODE expresses an entreaty:

Save my child!

Or a command:

Go!

When the subject of an imperative sentence is not given, the subject YOU is always understood.

A verb used as another part of speech is called a
VERBAL.

Most verbs are action words; they indicate actions.
But to the process of acting we can give a name.
When we want to *name* the action that a person
is taking or performing, we make a noun out of
the verb.

The man *eats* his dinner.

The *name* of the action the man is taking is
eating, or *to eat*. *Eating* and *to eat* are
nouns. We can say "Eating is fun" or
"To eat is necessary."

From the action a person is taking we can also make
an adjective to describe the person acting.

The *running* boy stumbled.

From the verb *runs* we make an adjective,
running. *Running* describes *boy*. *Running* is thus an adjective.

When we use a form of a verb as a noun or as an
adjective it is called a VERBAL.

There are three kinds of VERBALS. They are:

The INFINITIVE

The GERUND

The PARTICIPLE

When we say:

> *To see* is *to believe,*

we are making use of forms of the verbs *see* and *believe.* This form of the verb is called the INFINITIVE.

It is formed by placing the word *to* before the present tense verb.

The INFINITIVE is almost always used as a noun.*

To be, to see, to think, to know, to act, are all INFINITIVE forms. You can think of many more.

The INFINITIVE expresses no fixed time. It is timeless.

---

*Sometimes as in the following examples, infinitives at first glance seem to be adjectives or adverbs:

    Flee from the wrath *to come.*

  (*To come* seems to tell *what kind of* wrath, and thus to be an adjective.)

    He came *to sing.*

  (*To sing* seems to tell *why* he came, and thus to be an adverb.)

But the true explanation of these usages is that we use shortcuts in our speech and have come to leave out some words of

The GERUND is also a verbal noun.

> He was annoyed by the *barking* of the dog.

> In this sentence, *barking* is a form of the verb *bark,* but it is used as a noun and as the object of a preposition.

Barking $\left\{\begin{array}{l}\text{by } nature \text{ is a verb.} \\ \text{by } use \text{ is a noun.}\end{array}\right.$

Barking is a GERUND..

The GERUND is formed by adding *ing* to the present tense verb.

---

the sentence. The examples on the preceding page should probably be written:

> Flee from the wrath which is *to come.*

(*To come* is a noun, a predicate nominative after *which is.*)

> He came in order *to sing,* or
> He came for *to sing.*

(*To sing* is a noun, the object of a preposition. The use of the infinitive after *for* lingers in Mother Goose: "Simple Simon went a-fishing *for to catch* a whale." But in modern speech we leave out the preposition.)

A verbal noun is *always* used as a noun.

However, in a few cases the verbal noun, even though it has a *noun* use, has a strong *verb* flavor.

He disliked *writing letters.*

Writing is a verbal noun.

Letters is the object of the verbal noun *writing.*

Writing letters is the object of the verb *disliked.*

A PARTICIPLE is a verbal adjective.

Barking dogs never bite.

In this sentence, *barking* is a form of the verb *bark,* but it is used as an adjective describing *dogs.*

Barking { by *nature* is a verb.
{ by *use* is an adjective.

Barking is a PRESENT PARTICIPLE.

The PRESENT PARTICIPLE, like the GERUND, is formed by adding *ing* to the present tense verb.

If a word ending in *ing* is used as a *noun,* it is a GERUND; if it is used as an *adjective,* it is a PRESENT PARTICIPLE.

The PAST PARTICIPLE is formed by adding *d, ed, n,* or *t* to the present tense of the verb, except in the case of a few verbs which have irregular forms. It is also an adjective and its use is similar to that of the present participle.

The *chopped* wood lay in a pile.

The past participle, *chopped,* modifies the noun, *wood.*

The house is *deserted.*

The past participle, *deserted,* modifies the noun, *house.*

The *chosen* song was sung.

The past participle, *chosen,* modifies the noun, *song.*

Any participle with *having, having been,* or *being,* is called a COMPOUND PARTICIPLE.

Having spoken her mind, she closed the door.
Having been awakened, he turned off the alarm.
Being chased by a mad dog, he ran home.

vi

The Adverb

Something is done: the ADVERBS then
Tell *where,* and *why,* and *how,* and *when.*

 Like their first cousins, the adjectives, adverbs are gossips, too. They "tell on" verbs, adjectives, and other adverbs.

They tell:

where   why   how   when

	Answers question:
She is going *somewhere.*	*Where?*
Therefore you must go.	*Why?*
She spoke *quietly.*	*How?*
The horse will run *immediately.*	*When?*

67

More adverbs:

Where?	*Why?*
down	therefore
here	hence
there	wherefore
behind	why
forward	
somewhere	
where	
nowhere	

How?	*When?*
thus	never
hardly	now
nearly	often
not	always
so	ago
well	soon
yes	until
no	sometimes
certainly	when
willingly	immediately
quietly	

Usually a word ending in *ly* is an ADVERB.

Certain adverbs, such as *wholly, fatally, entirely,* can not be compared.

But most adverbs can be compared. They form their comparative and superlative degrees like adjectives of more than two syllables by using *more, most, less,* and *least.*

> least rapidly
> less rapidly
> rapidly
> more rapidly
> most rapidly

Comparison suggests that adverbs and adjectives, like a roller-coaster, have their ups and downs. The highest "ups" and the lowest "downs" are the superlatives. The positive is on the level. Between are the comparatives.

No
is an adverb.
Yes, YES is an adverb, too.

vii
The Preposition

A PREPOSITION precedes a noun:
By, at, from, to, or *in* the town.

Pre means *before.*

Preposition means a *before position.*

A PREPOSITION is a word that has a position before a noun or pronoun.

Like ushers, PREPOSITIONS go before, or lead in, nouns or pronouns.

on the ladder	above the window
at the game	beyond the river
from the barn	to the store

On, at, from, above, beyond, to, are PREPOSITIONS

A PREPOSITION shows *relation*.

This relation may be:

> position in time or space
> motion
> agency
> accompaniment
> purpose

Position in time or space
$\begin{cases} \text{at} \\ \text{near} \\ \text{in} \\ \text{on} \\ \text{between} \\ \text{from} \\ \text{about} \end{cases}$

Motion
$\begin{cases} \text{up} \\ \text{down} \\ \text{to} \\ \text{into} \\ \text{through} \end{cases}$

Agency $\begin{cases} \text{with} \\ \text{by} \\ \text{through} \end{cases}$ Accompaniment $\begin{cases} \text{with} \end{cases}$

Purpose $\begin{cases} \text{for} \end{cases}$

On   *Under*   *Above*   *Near*

The PREPOSITIONS show the *relation* of the book to the table.

Always look for the noun or pronoun that follows the preposition. We call this noun or pronoun the OBJECT OF THE PREPOSITION.

She danced *on* the *stage*.

Stage is the noun following the preposition *on*. Therefore, *stage* is the OBJECT OF THE PREPOSITION *on*.

Find the OBJECTS OF THE PREPOSITIONS in these sentences:

He laughed at the show.
The dog tugged at the strap.
He came into the house.
He floats through the air.
He crawled under the car.
He sang to her.

The PREPOSITION is a dictator word!

It *governs* its object.

The PREPOSITION *governs its object* by deciding with what word or phrase its object may associate.

> The house *by the road* was sold.

Road is the OBJECT OF THE PREPOSITION *by*. *By* determines that *road* shall associate with *house*.

Therefore we say that *by the road* is a PREPOSITIONAL PHRASE, used as an adjective to describe the noun *house*.

> *Up the hill* he rolled a rock.

Hill is the OBJECT OF THE PREPOSITION, *up*. *Up* determines that *hill* shall associate with *rolled*. *Rolled* is a verb. The only part of speech that can modify or describe a verb is an adverb.

Therefore the PREPOSITIONAL PHRASE, *up the hill*, is used as an adverb to modify or describe the verb, *rolled*.

Look closely at this sentence:

> Mary baked John a dumpling.

What did Mary bake?

The answer is *dumpling*. (It couldn't be John!)

What place does *John* have in this sentence?

Suppose we introduce the preposition *for*. Now we have:

> Mary baked a dumpling *for* John.

John is the OBJECT OF THE PREPOSITION *for*.

Another sentence:

> He sang Mary a song.

What place in the sentence does *Mary* have?

By introducing the preposition *to* we get:

> He sang a song *to* Mary.

Mary is the OBJECT OF THE PREPOSITION *to*.

When the prepositions *to* and *for* are left out, the nouns are called INDIRECT OBJECTS of the verb. Really, they are OBJECTS OF THE PREPOSITIONS, which are understood.

The INDIRECT OBJECT is another form of the OBJECTIVE CASE explained on page 18.

PREPOSITION is a long word, but many short words are prepositions.

Here are a few:

at	of
but	off
by	on
for	to
in	up

Here are some longer ones:

about	behind	over
above	below	save
across	beside	through
against	between	toward
along	beyond	under
amid	concerning	underneath
among	during	until
around	from	upon
atop	into	within
before	outside	without

Say to every preposition,
"What's your OBJECT?"

viii

The Conjunction

And, or, and *but* join words and clauses,
CONJUNCTIONS,—used instead of pauses.

Con means *together.*
Junction means a *joining.*
Conjunction means *that which joins together,* as a
bridge connecting two sides of a stream.

In grammar, a CONJUNCTION is a word that joins
or connects other words, phrases, clauses, or sentences.

words	bread *and* butter
phrases	up hill *and* down dale
clauses	The bird flew away *but* he returned.

Some conjunctions are:

and	besides
or	as
but	also
either	although
neither	though
nor	unless
because	yet
for	however
hence	moreover
after	nevertheless
if	so
even if	still
as if	in order that
whereas	lest
whether	provided
while	since
wherever	than
whenever	until

The Interjection

Strong-feeling words are *Ouch!* and *Oh!*
They're INTERJECTIONS: *Ah, Bah, Lo!*

Interject comes from two Latin words, meaning *to throw into.*

An INTERJECTION is a word *thrown into* a sentence, or *thrown among* other words, to express strong feeling.

An INTERJECTION adds spice and tang to writing and speech.

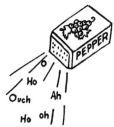

Oh! I wish I had known that.
Ah, there you are!
Alas! It's too late now.

When used as a part of the form of address, commonly in poetry or prayer, we use "O" instead of "Oh."

"Give me of your bark, O birch tree."

The INTERJECTION is an orphan word. It usually stands alone and has no grammatical connection with other words in the sentence.

x

The Sentence

"Grammar is the art of speaking words properly."
—Samuel Johnson

Why do you and I talk anyway? To *convey our thoughts* from our minds to the minds of others.

What do we use as conveyors? We use *words*.

We put words into PHRASES and CLAUSES, and these we fashion into SENTENCES.

Sometimes we use a single word:

John!

Fire!

Yes.

Of course, these words are really incomplete sentences. A part is understood. What we mean is:

John, come here.

Here is a fire!

Yes, I agree. (or) Yes, I will do it.

Sometimes we use PHRASES.

A PHRASE is a group of words in a sentence that
performs the duties of a noun, adjective, or adverb.

> *At the movie, in the boat, to the light-
> house, from the porch,* are PHRASES.
> Let us think of them as two-wheeled
> trailers.

> *To eat sparingly* is usually wise.

This phrase is used as a noun. It is the subject of the verb *is*.

> The man *in the moon* smiled.

In the moon is a phrase used as an adjective.
It describes *man*.

> The dog scooted *under the bed*.

This phrase is used as an adverb. It tells
about the verb *scooted*. It tells *where*.

Arriving at the airport, the travelers hurried to their plane.

Arriving at the airport is a phrase used as an adjective to describe *travelers.*

Within this phrase is another phrase. *At the airport* is a phrase used as an adverb to modify the participle *arriving.* It tells *where.*

Here is an assignment: Be a detective and find all the phrases in the following sentences. Tell what kind each is (noun, adjective, adverb), and what word it describes or modifies:

1. I sat by the road.
2. I looked at my watch.
3. She found a four-leaf clover near the hollyhocks.
4. From the watchman he learned the time.
5. The flag of our country is beautiful.
6. He dragged his tired feet up the stairs.
7. The circus is coming to town.
8. "To the top" was their motto.
9. Sitting by herself, she thought of a plan.

Sometimes we use CLAUSES.

A CLAUSE is a group of words that contains a subject and a predicate (makes a statement about a subject).

We can tell a PHRASE from a CLAUSE by the fact that a CLAUSE always contains a *verb*.

There are two kinds of CLAUSES: DEPENDENT (often called SUBORDINATE) and INDEPENDENT.

Subordinate comes from two Latin words: *sub,* meaning *below;* and *ordinis,* meaning *order* or *rank.*

Thus, *subordinate* means that the clause bearing this name is below the rank of the independent clause.

Dependent also comes from two Latin words: *de,* meaning *down from;* and *pendens,* meaning *hanging.*

If a DEPENDENT CLAUSE is hanging down from or fastened on something, what is it attached to?

It is attached to or dependent upon some word or words in the INDEPENDENT CLAUSE.

A DEPENDENT CLAUSE (or SUBORDINATE CLAUSE) is a *jack-of-all-trades*.

Like the PHRASE, a DEPENDENT CLAUSE sometimes does the work of a *noun*, sometimes the work of an *adjective*, and sometimes the work of an *adverb*.

That he talks too much is plain to me.

That he talks too much is the DEPENDENT CLAUSE. It is doing the work of a *noun*. It is used as the *subject* of the verb *is*.

I wish *that you would go home*.

That you would go home is the DEPENDENT CLAUSE. It is doing the work of a *noun*. It is used as the *direct object* of the verb *wish*.

The stream *that flowed by the house* is dry.

That flowed by the house is the DEPENDENT CLAUSE. It is doing the work of an adjective. It describes *stream*.

When the rain came, the ice melted.

When the rain came is the DEPENDENT CLAUSE. It is doing the work of an *adverb*. It modifies the verb *melted*. It answers the question, "When?"

Phrases and dependent clauses are *fragments* of the sentence.

The INDEPENDENT CLAUSE is the *important* part of the sentence.

An INDEPENDENT CLAUSE is not "hanging down from," not pulled along by, anything; it runs on its own power, so to speak. Often it tows a phrase or a dependent clause or one or more of each. Sometimes the INDEPENDENT CLAUSE tows many phrases and dependent clauses.

 We have thought of the PHRASE as a two-wheeled trailer, like the small trailer we sometimes fasten to the family car.

 Let us think of the DEPENDENT CLAUSE as a larger, four-wheeled trailer.

 Now, let us think of the INDE-PENDENT CLAUSE as the auto-mobile which pulls the trailers.

Phrases and dependent clauses are never complete in themselves. They do not run on their own power; they must be towed. They are always attached in some manner to an INDEPENDENT CLAUSE.

A sentence, to be a sentence, *must* contain one INDE-
PENDENT CLAUSE. It may contain two or more.
It may contain one or more DEPENDENT CLAUSES.
It may contain one or more PHRASES.

When in doubt about a clause, ask it, "Are you the
automobile or the four-wheeled trailer in this sentence? Can the sentence 'go' without you, or can
you 'go' without the rest of the sentence?"

If the clause can run by itself, it is the automobile.
The clause is INDEPENDENT. If the clause cannot
run by itself, it is a four-wheeled trailer, a DEPEND-
ENT CLAUSE.

> When the darkness came *I lighted the lamp.*
> If the rain stops *I shall take a walk.*
> While the band played *the girl sang.*

The clauses in italics are independent. They are the
cars that can run by themselves. The other clauses
are the dependent clauses that cannot run by themselves.

Often a sentence contains *only* an independent clause.

> The sun set.

Clauses may contain phrases.

> While the band played, the girl in the boat sang.
> *In the boat* is a phrase. *The girl in the boat sang*
> is an INDEPENDENT CLAUSE containing the phrase
> *in the boat.*

A SENTENCE consists of a subject and an assertion about that subject.

There are *three kinds of sentences:*

A SIMPLE SENTENCE states *one* fact or makes *one* inquiry about a fact. A SIMPLE SENTENCE contains one independent clause.

Birds fly.
Do choke-cherries choke, Jerry?
That radio screeches continually.

A COMPOUND SENTENCE states two or more facts, all equally important, and connected by *and, but,* or other conjunctions, or punctuation. A COMPOUND SENTENCE contains two or more independent clauses.

Bill built the fire and Bob pitched the tent.
Bill built the fire; Bob pitched the tent.

A COMPLEX SENTENCE states one principal or independent fact and one or more minor or dependent facts. A COMPLEX SENTENCE contains one independent clause and one or more dependent clauses.

The car skidded when the tire blew out.
The sun came out as the rain ceased.

A sentence can do one of *three* things:

1. State or assert
2. Ask a question
3. Give a command

A sentence that states or asserts or declares that something is true or is not true is called a DECLARATIVE SENTENCE.

> The cow jumped over the moon.
> The plane did not crash.

A sentence that asks if something *is* or *is not, was* or *was not, will be* or *will not be* is called an INTERROGATIVE SENTENCE.

Interrogative means *questioning, inquiring, asking.*
The interrogative sign is the question mark:

> Isn't Popeye a sailorman?
> Was the plane a new one?
> Will you be a worker or a shirker?

A sentence that commands or demands is called an IMPERATIVE SENTENCE.

> Wash your face.

XI

Punctuation

"For a reader that pointeth ill,
A good sentence oft may spill."
—Geoffrey Chaucer

Sentences, like traffic, have STOP and GO signals:

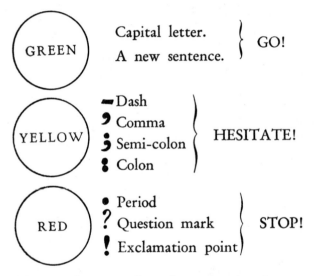

Observe these signals and you won't often go wrong
in sentence traffic.

Now a word about the APOSTROPHE.

The APOSTROPHE has two main uses:

1. It is used with the letter *s* to form the possessive case of nouns.

   a. With singular nouns the possessive is formed by the apostrophe followed by the letter *s:*
   The boy's shoe   John's hat

   b. With plural nouns not ending in *s* the possessive is formed in the same way:
   men's shirts   children's games

   c. With plural nouns ending in *s* the possessive is formed by adding the apostrophe:
   ladies' dresses   senators' wives

2. The apostrophe is also used to indicate the omission of one or more letters:

cannot	do not	have not	over	it is
can't	don't	haven't	o'er	it's

As a pronoun is a stand-in for a noun, an apostrophe used in this way is a stand-in for one or more letters.

A Few Common Errors

"If you speak three words it shall three times report you."
—Francis Bacon

A poem tells us that
    "The Gingham Dog and the Calico Cat
    Side by side on the table sat."
Finally they *ate each other up!*
Two negatives in the same sentence do the *same thing!*
    They eat each other up.
For example:
    She does not like no worms,
really means:
    She *likes* worms.

                    It is me
may be correct according to common usage,
                        but
                    It is me
will never be correct according to English grammar.
Always say
                    It is I.

It's time to talk about *its* and *it's*.

Its and *it's* are often misused.

The difference lies in the use of the apostrophe.

When *its* is used as a pronoun, the apostrophe is *never* used.

The flower lost its fragrance.
The day ran its course.

When *it's* is used as a contraction of *it is*, the apostrophe is *always* used.

> It's a great day for the Irish!
> It's three o'clock in the morning.

It's really quite simple, isn't it? Just remember the apostrophe and its proper use.

Can and *may* are often misused because their uses are
not clearly understood.

> Can I be an opera singer?
> Can we walk that far?
> Can I learn to ski?

Can tells or asks about a person's *ability* to do a certain thing.

You will associate the words *can* and *able* more easily
if you repeat these words four or five times:

> can   able
> Cain   Abel

You will remember it now!

> May I borrow your book, please?
> May I look at your funny paper?
> You may.

May gives or asks *permission* to do a certain thing.
If *please* belongs in the question, then *may*
belongs in both question and answer.

Who knows how to use *who* and *whom* properly?

REMEMBER: The relative pronoun, *who,* like the personal pronouns, has different forms for different cases.

Nominative case   *who*
Possessive case   *whose*
Objective case   *whom*

The possessive case gives little trouble. We say:

That is the man *whose* window was broken.

It is confusion between the nominative form, *who,* and the objective form, *whom,* that leads us into difficulty. It is necessary, therefore, to decide, before we use the pronoun, what is properly its use in the sentence.

Relative pronouns, although they agree with their antecedents in person, gender, and number (like all pronouns), take their *case* because of their relationship with a verb or a preposition in the sentence.

The girl *who* was skating has slipped and fallen.

The relative pronoun, *who,* stands for its antecedent, *girl,* and really agrees with it in gender, number, and person. But in its own little clause, *who was skating,* the relative pronoun, *who,* is clearly the *subject of the verb,* and must, therefore be in the nominative case.

This is the woman *whom* I assisted.

The case of the relative pronoun, *whom*, is set by its relationship to the verb in the clause, *whom I assisted*. The clause says, *I assisted whom*. The relative pronoun is the *direct object of the verb, assisted*, and is in the objective case.

She is the girl *whom* I was waiting for.

The relative clause says, *I was waiting for whom. Whom* is the *object of the preposition, for*, and is in the objective case.

Always watch for parenthetical words in the relative clause. Such words are often misleading and cause many errors in the use of relative pronouns. For example, in the sentence,

He is the man *who* I expect will obtain the
nomination,

the temptation is to make the relative pronoun the object of *expect*, and to use *whom*. But the words, *I expect*, are really parenthetical and have no grammatical relationship with the relative pronoun. The clause says, *who will obtain the nomination. Who* is therefore in the nominative case, standing for the particular *man* about whom the sentence is talking.

But notice what happens if we change the relative clause and put the emphasis upon the words *I expect.*

Whom do you expect to win the game?

The main verb of the relative clause is *expect,* and the relative pronoun becomes the subject of the infinitive *to win.*

The subject of the infinitive is always in the objective case.

Whom is, therefore, properly used. The clause says, *You expect whom to win the game.*

The rules for *who* and *whom* also govern the use of the compound forms, *whoso, whoever,* and *whosoever.*

Now, who can tell whom how to use who?

In the case of *shall* and *will*, "I" and "we" stand
alone, like the farmer in the dell.

I shall   we shall
you will   you will
he, she, it will   they will

These are the forms we use when we say something
will take place in the future. This is the way the
simple future of verbs is expressed.

When evening comes I shall go home.
You will be ten years old tomorrow.
They will come with me.
When shall we three meet again?
Friends, you will not see me tomorrow.
My parents will be pleased with my progress.

Review the simple future of verbs on page 51.

Now, when *determination* is to be expressed, we use just the opposite forms.

I will!	We will!
You shall!	You shall!
He, she, it shall!	They shall!

These are the forms we use when we say something *must* take place in the future.

This is the way determination is expressed.

> I will attend to the matter at once.
> You shall not go.
> She shall have music wherever she goes.
> We will fight to the last man.
> I have given orders that you shall be freed.
> They shall not pass.

Should and *would* follow the same rules as *shall* and *will*.

Why let *lie* and *lay* lie around without learning their
proper places?

First, review, briefly, transitive and intransitive verbs
on pages 41-43.

Lie is *intransitive*. It takes no object.

Its forms are:

PRESENT TENSE	PRESENT PARTICIPLE	PAST TENSE	PAST PARTICIPLE
lie	lying	lay	lain

The book lies on the table.

The lion is lying down.

The dog lay down.

For months the groundhog has lain in his shelter.

These words cannot be used in the passive voice.

Why?

Lay is a *transitive* verb. It must have an object.

Lay can be used in both active and passive voice.
Its forms are:

PRESENT TENSE	PRESENT PARTICIPLE	PAST TENSE	PAST PARTICIPLE
lay	laying	laid	laid

Active **voice** { The hen lays an egg.
John is laying a walk.
The hen laid an egg.

Passive voice { An egg was laid by the hen.
The walk was laid by John.

Confusion of *lie* and *lay* often occurs because the
present tense of *lay* is spelled like the past tense
of *lie*.

Let's set ourselves right on *sit* and *set*.

The difference between them is like that between *lie* and *lay*.

Sit is the *intransitive* verb. It does not take an object and cannot be used in the passive voice.

Sit means the act of sitting and nothing more.

Its forms are:

PRESENT TENSE	PRESENT PARTICIPLE	PAST TENSE	PAST PARTICIPLE
sit	sitting	sat	sat

I sit in the sun.

She is sitting in the hammock.

He sat up and listened.

They sat through two shows.

They have sat through two shows.

Sit just *sits*.

Set, in the sense of putting something somewhere or acting upon something, is a *transitive* verb. It takes an object. It may be used in either the active or passive voice.

Its forms are:

PRESENT TENSE	PRESENT PARTICIPLE	PAST TENSE	PAST PARTICIPLE
set	setting	set	set

> She set the dishes on the table.
> The furniture was set on the floor.
> I was setting the table.

BUT, *set* is sometimes intransitive, as when we say:

> The sun sets behind the clouds.
> The traveler set out again upon his journey.

Some dos and don'ts for using *do* and *does*.

Use *do* or *don't* with the pronouns *I, you, we,* and
they, and with plural nouns.

I do	or	I don't
you do	or	you don't
we do	or	we don't
they do	or	they don't
children do	or	children don't
elephants do	or	elephants don't

Use *does* and *doesn't* with the pronouns *he, she, it,* and with singular nouns.

he does	or	he doesn't
she does	or	she doesn't
it does	or	it doesn't
the hippo does	or	the hippo doesn't

Remember, correct
usage includes correct
pronunciation.

Here are:

ELEVEN COMMANDMENTS OF GOOD SPEECH

Say *just*, not *jist* or *jest*.
Say *I think not*, not *I don't think*.
Never say *ain't* or *hain't*.
Say *he doesn't*, not *he don't*.
Say *because*, not *becuz*.
Say *hundred*, not *hunderd*.
Say *again*, not *agin*.
Say *going to*, not *gonna*.
Say *for*, not *fur*.
If you mean *picture*, do not say *pitcher*.
Say *library*, not *liberry*.

xiii

Roundup and Review

"Lasso those wild words lest the sentence throw you."

We have learned that all our speech and all our writing is made up of only eight kinds of words. We have learned what these kinds of words are and something about the way in which we use them.

We come now to the Roundup, a roundup of *words*.

Let us, in our minds, throw a lasso or lariat around each one of the herd of words in the following sentences, and put them all in the corral, every one branded with the name of the part of speech to which it belongs:

1. The frost nipped her nose.
2. She drank her milk hurriedly.
3. Skating is a popular sport.
4. The performer dropped his hat, and the clown picked it up and ran.
5. Honesty is the best policy.
6. The old, ragged dollar bill was lost.
7. "To be, rather than to seem:" this is our motto.
8. Ouch! The shoe pinches.
9. The green turtle stopped in the dusty road.
10. Apple pie and cheese go well together.
11. The stout man's hat blew off.
12. No. She is not at home.
13. "The time has come," the Walrus said, "to speak of many things."
14. Sylvia Ann and Kiki delivered apples, corn, and tomatoes to Miss Hayes.
15. He saw the home of George Washington at Mount Vernon, and visited the White House in the nation's capital city.
16. A thing of beauty is a joy forever.
17. The applause of the audience made it impossible to hear the voice of the speaker.
18. This is the forest primeval, the murmuring pines and the hemlocks.
19. Strike while the iron is hot.
20. Oh! John has slipped on the ice.

| PHRASES | DEPENDENT CLAUSES | INDEPENDENT CLAUSES |

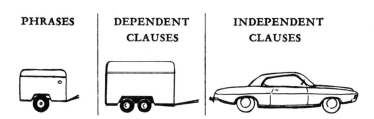

On a separate sheet of paper draw, as above, a two-wheeled trailer, a big house-trailer, and an automobile.

1. Now break up the following sentences into phrases, dependent clauses, and independent clauses. On the separate sheet of paper, write the PHRASES in a column under the two-wheeled trailer. Write the DEPENDENT CLAUSES under the four-wheeled trailer. Write the INDEPENDENT CLAUSES under the automobile.

2. Next, tell how each fragment of the sentence in the two "trailer" columns is used (as a noun, adjective, or adverb).

3. Explain to what word or group of words in the independent clause each fragment of the sentence (two-wheeled or four-wheeled trailer) is attached. (Remember that many autos have no trailers, and that some sentences have no fragments, no phrases or independent clauses.)

4. If the sentence-fragments in the trailer columns are used as adverbs, explain what question each answers (how, when, where, or why).

1. Jake stubbed his toe.
2. Jerry caught a big pike.
3. Between here and there the buses run.
4. She gave a doughnut to the small boy.
5. That she was often late to her classes caused her instructors much annoyance.
6. Into the air the ball went sailing high.
7. He thinks that riding horseback is fun.
8. John studied arithmetic and Joe read history.
9. The farmer ploughed his fields while his son dragged them.
10. She asked the milkman on the route to bring her three quarts of milk.
11. Listen to that bird scolding his mate.
12. In order that he may be permitted to vote, each citizen must register in advance at the polling place.
13. The proper study of mankind is man.
14. Under the spreading chestnut tree, the village smithy stands.
15. This is the rat that ate the malt that lay in the house that Jack built.

What kind of a sentence is each of the following?
a. Simple, complex, or compound?
b. Declarative, interrogative, or imperative?

1. The owl slept.
2. The owl yawned and stretched herself.
3. The owl flew away when the sun came up.
4. Mary and Carrie washed the blackboards.
5. While Mother Robin sat on the nest, Father Robin hunted worms.
6. Sarah and Tillie made a doll's hat and a doll's coat.
7. Did Mrs. Jones drive the car while Mr. Jones dozed?
8. Who put salt in my coffee?
9. Class, stand.
10. Sing the song softly.
11. Jack Sprat could eat no fat; his wife could eat no lean.
12. Have you chosen your class flower?
13. No.
14. This is the spot where I stood, and there is the tree in which I saw the birds.
15. Bury the hatchet, boys.
16. October first comes after September thirtieth.
17. When the entertainment is ended and the last guest has departed, I shall put out the lights and lock the doors.
18. The Assyrian came down like a wolf on the fold.

And Here Are Games

"Joking and humor are pleasant, and often of extreme utility."
—Cicero

ALL RIGHT! ALL RIGHT!

Materials: A tin frying pan and a ruler to which a wad of cotton has been fastened.

Each player is called upon to recite a stanza from the poem, "Parts of Speech," on pages 2 and 3. Those reciting stanzas correctly, bang the frying pan twice with the ruler. Those failing to recite correctly, lose their bangs and must await a new turn.

110

POPPING CORN

The eight parts of speech are written in large letters across the blackboard. Before each word stands a pupil holding a sheet of white paper.

A sentence is read slowly before the game begins. After the signal, "Ready," the sentence is read again. At the first word, the pupil standing before that part of speech, holds the sheet of paper on his head and jumps as high as possible. The pupil standing before the next part of speech called does the same, and so on. If one of the "kernels" cannot pop, he gives up his place to someone else and must stand on the side lines with an eraser on his head.

THE MUSIC GOES 'ROUND AND 'ROUND

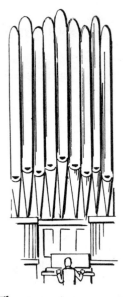

This game might also be called the Human Pipe Organ Game.

Nine pupils are chosen, each given a sheet of paper with one of the parts of speech printed in large letters on it. The pupils stand in a row and hold these names in front of them.

Another pupil, chosen to act as organist, stands in front of the group. The teacher gives a sentence, as, for example:
"The apples were red."

The organist goes to the ARTICLE as quickly as he can get there and touches him on the head. The ARTICLE bends slightly at the knees and then comes back into place as soon as the organist removes his hand. The organist is away as quickly as possible to the noun, verb and adjective, the action being repeated each time.

Another organist is then chosen!

Another tune!

PASS THE HAT

Write on a large piece of paper in
large letters any *noun*.

Let every member of the class see it.

Fold it and put it in a hat.

Let everyone write on a small piece of paper an adjective to fit the noun.

Have someone pass the hat.

Let everyone *throw* in or *at* the noun his or her
adjective.

Let them be read.

STATION F-U-N

Material: An improvised microphone

At the close of the recitation choose two
    pupils. One acts as the announcer who
    opens and closes the broadcast; the
    other, the speaker, gives the highlights
    of the grammar lesson for that day.

Frequent   broadcasting   over   Station
    F-U-N is suggested.

CHECK AND DOUBLE CHECK

Choose three persons:

> One to ask questions
> One to answer questions
> One to keep score

The scorekeeper takes his place at the blackboard. The other two persons stand before the class.

The questioner asks the other player a question concerning some fact in grammar.

Example:

> "What part of speech is the word *often?*"

If the person answers correctly, the scorekeeper gives him a check.

He is asked two more questions by the questioner. If he answers them correctly he is given double check. He then becomes the questioner and the questioner becomes the scorekeeper. Another person is chosen from the class to answer the questions. And the questioning goes on and on.

PUNCTUATION COURT

Prepare red, yellow, and green traffic tags for errors in punctuation.

Make a list, from compositions, of punctuation offenders.

One pupil acts as judge.

Another pupil acts as officer to present the traffic tags.

A third pupil acts as clerk and declares Punctuation Court to be in session.

A fourth pupil acts as officer to bring offenders before the court, one at a time.

Judge: "John Jones, you are charged with the serious offense of passing a period." (He is handed his paper with the error plainly marked.) "How do you plead, guilty or not guilty?" If he pleads not guilty he should state his reasons. If he pleads guilty he is sentenced to re-write the sentence correctly five times.

Never suspend sentence!

Call the next case.

Adjourn court!

INDEX